ATTENDANT OPERATOR

OBJECTIVE QUESTION ANSWERS

MANOJ DOLE

Copyright © Manoj Dole
All Rights Reserved.

Digitization is the need of the time. In the future, training in industrial training institutes will
need to be conducted using online internet to make training more convenient and easy. E-books
containing a set of MCQ questions will be made available to the trainees as they need to be
more accustomed to the multiple choice questions MCQ to prepare for the online exams taking
place in their industrial training institutes.

With all these factors in mind, Mr. Manoj Madhukar Dole Instructor, Industrial
Training Institute, Satara, has written books according to the new annual system and NSQF-5
syllabus. And they've created theoretical mobile apps and blogs to make training easier, and
made all these educational materials available for download on the world famous websites
Google Play Store, Amazon and Apple Book Store.

The books were published by Hon'ble Joint Director Shri Rajendra Ghume Saheb
Regional Office of Vocational Education and Training, Pune on 9/1/2019, at this time Shri
Prakash Saigavkar Saheb Principal Government Industrial Training Institute Aundh Pune,
Shri Tukaram Misal Saheb Principal Govt. Q. Sanstha Satara, Shri Sachin Dhumal Saheb
District Vocational Education and Training Officer Satara, Shri Yatin Pargaonkar Saheb
Principal Govt. Q. Sanstha Kolhapur, Shri Vikas Teke Saheb Inspector Vocational Education
and Training Regional Office Pune, Palekar Foods Products Pvt. Ltd. Entrepreneurial Chairman
of Satara Mr. Nilkanthrao Palekar Saheb, Chairman of Hira Foods Mr. Ibrahim Baba Tamboli

Saheb, Mrs. Shalmali Pawar Headmaster Government Technical School Center Satara and
other dignitaries were present on the occasion.

Contents

Prologue

Attendant Operator is a simple e-Book for ITI & Engineering Course Attendant Operator (Chemical Plant). It contains objective questions with underlined & bold correct answers MCQ covering all topics including all about the latest & Important about Hack-sawing, marking, punching, Chiseling, Filing, Drilling, countersinking, counter boring, reaming, Taping, melting point, boiling point, compare properties of metals & alloys, Fire extinguisher, pipe joints, fittings valves on pipes, dismantling, overhauling, cleaning &assembling valves, centrifugal pump, gear pump, metering pump, screw pump, multistage compressor, fluid flow, heat transfer and mass transfer operations, Shell and tube Heat exchangers, evaporators, Distillation columns, manufacturing processes and pressure vessels, petroleum refining, Solvent extraction, Leaching, Absorption, Crystallization, and Drying, Size reduction, mixing conveying, and filtration, chemical reactor, plant utilities- steam, cooling tower, chilled water and lots more.

We add new question answers with each new version. Please email us in case of any errors/omissions. This is arguably the largest and best e-Book for All engineering multiple choice questions and answers.

As a student you can use it for your exam prep. This e-Book is also useful for professors to refresh material.

Foreword

Vocational education and training is imparted through the Department of Vocational Education
and Training through the Department of Business Education and Business Practical to supply
multi-skilled artisans in line with the rapidly growing demand in the industrial sector in the
21st century. All the occupations within the institutions are important, as the trainees from
these occupations develop multi-skills as per the demands of the industry.

with the noble intention of making available MCQ e-books suitable for all businesses,
considering that all the examinations in all the industries in the industrial sector are conducted
online and include MCQ method questions. Mr. Manoj Madhukar Dole has written a very good
e-book on MCQ method as per the new annual syllabus. This e-book will definitely be a guide
for all the trainees, trainee candidates, training instructors and others concerned.

The author of the book is Mr. Manoj Madhukar Dole, Instructor Gov. ITI Satara has 17
years of training experience. Written as a new annual pattern, this e-book incorporates modern
digital QR Code technology to understand the layout, simple language, and simple syntax,
diagrams and videos for each subject. So I am sure that this e-book will definitely be useful for
in-depth study and exam practice. The work they have done is certainly commendable.

Mr. Tukaram Misal
Principal Government Industrial Training Institute Satara.

Preface

DGET New Delhi and CSTARI Kolkata have been implementing an annual pattern for all
businesses in ITI since the August 2018 session. The examination system will also be changed
and it will be online from this year and since all the questions are of Objective Type (MCQ), the
trainees are in dire need of in-depth study. It is with this in mind that we are delighted to
present the books based on the old NIMI pattern and a complete overview of the new annual
pattern, and we hope that these books will be a guide for all business directors and trainees. Is.

For writing these books, Johar Awate Saheb, Principal of ITI Akluj. Former
Principal of ITI Satara Saigavkar Saheb, Assistant Director Shri Chandrakant Dhekne Saheb
Regional Office of Vocational Education and Training, Pune, District Vocational Education and
Training Officer Sachin Dhumal Saheb and Headmaster Government Technical School Kendra
Shalmali Pawar Madam and son Adhiraj Dole, mother Kusum Dole, I am very grateful to my
father Madhukar Dole and wife Ashwini Dole for their special guidance and cooperation from
time to time.

Also, in a very short period of time, the book was reviewed by Shri Rajendra Ghume
Saheb, Joint Director, Vocational Education and Training Regional Office, Pune, for his
invaluable time in publishing the book. I am sincerely grateful for their feedback.

I am grateful to the Instructor of ITI Satara for there continuous support from the
very beginning of writing the book.

From this book, I consider myself blessed to have shared my thoughts on e-learning
with you. I will not claim that this book is perfect, because considering the perfection, this book
is an attempt and is in its infancy. They will be valuable for improvement if they are tested and
suggested.

Manoj Dole
Dated 9/1/2019

CHAPTER I

Attendant Operator MCQ

01] In case of bleeding, take treatment Of

D] cold 3" and rest

<u>A] spray cold water</u>

B] Bandage immediately -----.

B] Enquire about the accident thought treatment

02] in case of an accident, the victim should im

A] Asked to take rest

<u>C] Attended immediately</u>

D] leave him

03] First aid is given to an injured or ill person primarily....

A] Save life

B] Prevent further deterioration of the muff's

C] Give best possible comfort

<u>D] All of these</u>

04] Colour code for Bins for waste paper segregation is -----

<u>A] blue Colour</u>

B] Yellow Colour

C] Red Colour

D] Green Colour

05] In Japanese Seiko stands for --------------

<u>A] Shine</u>

B] Sort

C] Standardize

D] Sustain

06] Benefit of SS system is ------

A] Increase in productivity

B] Increase in quality

C] Reduction in wastage of time

<u>D] All of these</u>

03] SAFETY PRECAUTION 09

07] Safety is -----------

A] nobody's business

<u>B] every bodise business</u>

C] Some bodies business

D] The organization business

08] For basic categories of safety signs are available The meaning of"prohibition" sign ----

<u>A] shows it must not be done</u>

B] Shows what must be done

C] Warns the hazard or danger

D] Gives information of safety provision

09] Which one is a workshop safety?

<u>A] Keep shop floor clean and free from grease, oil or other slippery materials</u>

B] Stop the machine before changing the speed

C] Don't use cracked or chipped tools

D] Don't try to stop a running machine with hand

10] In Personal Protect Equipment (PPE] HELMET is used to

<u>A] protect head</u>

B] Protect eyes

C] Protect hands

D] Protect ears

11] Which of the following belongs to general safety?

A Have a worker in good attitude

B] The work clean and clear

C] Concentrate on your work

<u>D] Keep the floor and gangways clean and clear</u>

12] While grinding, which is used to protect the eyes?

A] Dark green glass

B] Mask

C] Sun glasses

<u>D] Safety goggles</u>

13] Which of the following is done for machine safety?

<u>A] Check the oil level before starting the machine</u>

B] Do things in a methodical way

C] Keep the floor and gangways clean and clear

D] Don't use dies and scarves

14] In Personal Protect Equipment (PPE], 'sleeves' is used to protect ----------

A] Face

B] Eyes

C] Ears

D] Hands

15] ABC stands for --------------

A] Automatic Breathing Control

B] Automatic Blood Control

C] Airway Breathing Circulation

D] Automatic Blood Circulation

04] Fire & FIRE EXTINGUISHERS

16] To put off"Class B" fire, the types of fire extinguisher used is ....

A] dry power

B] Carbon dioxide

C] Jet of water

D] Foam type

17] Which type of fire extinguisher is used to put off general fire?

A] Water type Extinguisher

B] Foam type Extinguisher

C] Dry chemical powder Extinguisher

D] Carbon dioxide (C02] Extinguisher

18] One micrometer (U] is equal to...

A] 0.1mm

B] 0.01mm

C] 0.001mm

D] 0.0001mm

19] The caliper meant for measuring the width of a slot is...

A] Odd leg caliper

B] Outside caliper

C] Jenny caliper

D] Inside calliper

20] The size of the dividers are specified by the -----------

A] Total length of legs

B] Distance between the points when fully opened

C] Length of legs without points

D] distance between the pivot and the point

21] The instrument used to mark parallel lines, parallel to the datum edge is -

A] jenny caliper

B] Divider

C] Outside calliper

D] Inside calliper

22] Which one of the following is an indirect measuring tool?

A] Outside caliper

B] Vernier calliper

C] Steel rule

D] Outside micrometer

23] For cutting thin tubing, the most suitable pitch of the hacksaw blade is...

A] 1.8mm

B] 1.4mm

C] 1mm

D] 0.8mm

24] For cutting solid brass, the most suitable pitch of the hacksaw blade is...

A] 1.8mm

B] 1.4mm

C] 1mm

D] 0.8mm

25] A new hacksaw blade after a few strokes becomes loose because of the...

A] Stretching of the blade

B] Wing-nut threads being worn out

C] Wrong pitch of the blade

D] Improper selection of the set of saws.

26] While cutting small diameter pipes, it is advisable to watch regularly and ensure that...

A] The cut is along the curved line

B] More saw teeth are in contract

C] The work is not overheated

D] Proper balancing of hacksaw is maintained

27] The vice clamps are used to...

A] Protect hard jaws

B] Clamp the work pieces rigidly

C] Protect the finished surfaces

D] Prevent the movable jaw being filed

28] The reference surface during marking is provided by the...

A] Surface gauge

B] Workpiece

C] Drawing of the work

D] <u>Marking table surface</u>

29] The size of an engineer's vice is specified by the...

A] Length of the movable jaw

B] <u>Width of the jaws</u>

C] Height of the vice

D] Maximum opening of the jaws

30] The part of the universal surface gauge which helps to draw a parallel line along a datum edge is the..

A] Rocker arm

B] Snug

C] Fine adjustment screw

D] <u>Guide pins</u>

31] Scribers are made of...

A] Mild steel

B] <u>High carbon steel</u>

C] Brass

D] Cast iron

32] Portion of the hammer used for fixing the handle is...

A] Face

B] Peen

C] Cheek

D] <u>Eye hole</u>

33] Weight of the hammer for the marking purpose is...

A] <u>250g</u>

B] 500g

C] 1 kg

D] 2 kgs

34] The size of the dividers are specified by the...

A] Total length of the legs

B] Distance between the points when fully opened

C] Length of legs without the points

D] <u>Distance between the pivot and the point</u>

35] The included angle of the groove of 'V' block is always....

A] 45°

B] 60°

C] 90°

D] <u>120°</u>

36] 'V' blocks are available in grades of...

A] <u>A & B</u>

B] A,B & C

C] 1,2 & 3

D] 1 & 2

37] 'V' blocks of grade 'B' are made of

A] <u>Cast iron</u>

B] Mild steel

C] Steel

D] Cast steel

38] Name the punch used to locate the centre.

A] Prick punch 30°

B] Prick punch 60°

<u>C] Centre punch</u>

D] Dot punch

39] The point angle of centre punch is --------

A] 30°

B] 50°

<u>c] 900</u>

D] 1200

40] Punches are used for forming ---------of any shape

<u>A] Holes</u>

B] Mining

C] Knurling

D] Reaming

41] Generally the length of the handle of the vice is ----------

A] 1.5 times the normal size of the vice

<u>B] 2.5 times the normal size of the vice</u>

C] 3.5 times the normal size of the vice

D] 4.5 times the normal size of the vice

42] Bench vice spindle is made of ....

<u>A] mild steel</u>

B] Cast iron

C] Tool steel

D] Bronze

43] The convexity of files helps...

A] To file concave surfaces

B] To file convex surfaces

C] <u>To prevent rounding of edges of work</u>

D] The file to become straight when pressure is applied

44] Which file used for filling wood, leather and other soft material? .

A] Single cut file

B] Double cut file

c] <u>Rasp cut file</u>

D] Curved cut file

45] File used is used for ------------

A] Cleaning the work piece

C] Renewing the file teeth

B] <u>cleaning the file teeth</u>

D] Cleaning the chips

46] File card is used to --------

A] Clean the work piece

C] Renew the file teeth

B] <u>Clean the file teeth</u>

47] The point angle of scriber is -----------

A] 30°

B] 60°

C] 5° to 10°

D] <u>12° to 15°</u>

48] The least count of vernier calliper is (main scale = 49 division, vernier scale = 50 division]

A] 0.1 mm

B] 0.01 mm

C] 0.001 mm

D] <u>0.02 mm</u>

49] The type of measurement made by using a Vernier Calliper is -------

A] Direct measurement

B] <u>Indirect measurement</u>

C] 90"] (a] 81 (b]

D] None of these

50] The least count of a vernier height gauge in the metric system is

A] 0.05 mm

B] 0.1 mm

C] <u>0.02 mm</u>

D] 0.001 mm

51] The least count of a vernier height gauge in the british system is

A] 0.05"

B] 0.001"

C] 0.002"

D] 1"

52] For marking purposes, a vernier height gauge must be used on the

A] bed of a machine tool

B] surface plate

C] square block

D] any flat surface

53] The reading of a vernier height gauge is similar to that of a

A] vernier caliper

B] depth micrometer

C] dial test indicator

D] gauge

54] The part which slides on the beam of a vernier height gauge is known

as a

A] base

B] beam scale

C] scriber

D] vernier slide

55] The size of a vernier height gauge is specified by the

A] height of the vernier scale

B] height of the beam

C] width of the beam

D] size of the base

56] The base of the vernier height gauge is generally made out of

A] cast iron

B] steel

C] aluminium alloy

D] tungsten carbide

57] Accuracy or least count of a metric outside micrometer is ---------

A] 0-1 mm

B] 0.01 mm

C] 0.001 mm

D] 0.02 mm

58] 1000 microns means -----

A] 1 mm

B] 1 m

C] 1000 mm

D] 10 cm

59] in a metric micrometer, a complete revolution of thimble advances ------------

A] 0.01 mm

B] 0.25 mm

C] 0.50 mm

D] 100mm

60] Ratchet Stop in the micrometer helps to ------------

A] Control the pressure

B] lock the spindle

C] Adjust the zero error

D] Hold the work piece

61] 1000 micron means ------------

A] 1 mm

B] 1 m

C] 1000 mm

D] 10 cm

62] What is the zero reading of a 50-75 mm outside micrometer?

A] 0000 mm

B] 001 mm

C] 2500 mm

D] 5000 mm

63] The value of the smallest division on sleeve of a metric outside micrometer is -----

A] 050 mm

B] 100 mm

C] 150 mm

D] 200 mm

64] Ratchet stop in the micrometer helps to ---------

A] control the pressure

B] Lock the spindle

C] Adjust the zero error

D] Hold the work piece

65] The least count of a vernier bevel protractor is

A] 1"

B] 5'

C] 1°

D] 5 ∘

66] The part of a vernier bevel protractor which is normally used as a reference base for measuring angles is the

A] Blade

B] <u>Stock</u>

C] Disc

C] Main scale

67] The part of a vernier bevel protector on which main scale divisions are marked is the

A] Stock

B] Dial

C] <u>Disc</u>

D] Adjustable blade

68] The part of a bevel protractor, which comes in contact with the inclined surface while measuring is the

A] <u>Blade</u>

B] Stock

C] Disc

D] Dial

69] The value of each division of the main scale of a vernier bevel protractor is

A] 5'

B] <u>1∘</u>

C] 5∘

D]10∘

70] The value of each division of the vernier scale of a bevel protractor is

A] 1∘

B] 1∘5'

C] <u>1∘55'</u>

D] 5'

71] The taper shank drills are held on the machine by means of

A] Chucks

<u>B] Sleeves</u>

C] Drift

D] Vice

72] Drill chucks are fitted on the drilling machine spindle by means of a

A] Knurled ring

B] Arbor

C] Drift

D] Pinion and key

73] The Morse taper provided on drills ranges between

A] MT 1 to MT 5

B] MT 1 to MT 4

C] MT 0 to MT 5

D] MT 0 to MT 4

74] A drift is used for

A] Drawing a drill location

B] Fixing chuck on the machine spindle

C] Removing a broken drill from the work

D] Removing the drill from the machine spindle

75] When the taper shank of the drill is larger than the machine spindle, the device to hold the drill is a

A] Drill sleeve

B] Taper socket

C] Drill drift

D] Chuck and key

76] The suitable cutting fluid for drilling mild steel in a drilling machine is

A] Synthetic soluble oil

B] Neat oil

C] Distilled water

D] Soluble oil

77] A special feature of the radial drilling machine is

A] It can be used for drilling with a HSS drill

B] Table can be moved and set at any position

C] A variety of speeds is available

D] The spindle can be brought to any position

78] The point angle of drills depends on

A] The size of the drill

B] The type of machine

C] The material of the work

D] The RPM of the drill

79] The point angle for a standard drill is

A] 60°

B] 108°

C] <u>118°</u>

D] 135°

80] The helical angle determines the

A] Cutting angle

B] Chew angle

C] <u>Rake angle</u>

D] Lip angle

81] The clearance angle of the drill is between

A] 3° to 5°

B] <u>8° to 12°</u>

C] 12° to 20°

D] 15° to 20°

82] In a remote place (no electricity available] a rail track is to be drilled Choose the right drilling machine

A] Radial drilling machine

B] Pillar drilling machine

C] <u>Ratchet drilling machine</u>

D] Sensitive drilling Machine

83] A drilling machine used by a carpenter for cabinet making is a

A] Ratchet drilling machine

B] Radial drilling machine

C] <u>Breast drilling machine</u>

D] Sensitive drilling machine

84] Which one of the following drilling machines is used for drilling holes where electricity is not available?

A] Bench drilling machine

B] Pillar drilling machine

C] Redial drilling machine

D] <u>Ratchet drilling machine</u>

85] Which one of the following drilling machine is used for heavy duty work?

A] Bench drilling machine

B] Pillar drilling machine

C] <u>Radial drilling machine</u>

D] Electric hand drilling machine

86] Drill chuck are held on the machine spindle by means of ------

A] arbor
B] Drift
C] draw-in bar
D] Chuck nut
87] Different speeds are obtained in a sensitive bench drilling machine by ----
A] Belt pulley mechanism
B] Hydraulic mechanism
C] Rack and Pinion mechanism
D] Cam and follower mechanism
88] Tap are re sharpened by grinding -----
A] Hutes
B] Threads
C] Diameter
D] Relief
89] The tapping drill size for M10 x 15 is ----------
A] 82
B] 83
C] 84
D] 85
90] A nut is to be made for a screw of M10XIS What should be the size of drilled hole?
A] 8-5 mm
B] 90 mm
C] 95 mm
D] 100 mm
91] The process of enlarging the end of a hole for accommodating the socket screw head is
A] Reaming
B] Spot facing
C] Counter boring
92] Appropriate tool used for spot facing operation is
A] Reamer
B] Counter sinks
C] Fly cutters
93] A short reamer with an axial hole used with an arbor or mandrel is called -------
A] Parallel reamer

B] Adjustable reamer

C] Expansion reamer

D] Chucking reamer

94] Which one of the following machine reamers is used to correct the misalignment between the reamer axis and the work axis?

A] Floating blade reamer

B] Machine jig reamer

C] Shell reamer

D] Chucking reamer

95] The depth of cut for metric square threading is

A] 06 x P

B] 05 x P

C] 05412 x P

D] 06412 x P

96] To cut buttress thread, the depth of cut is

A] 05412 x P

B] 06 x P

C] 07 x P

D] 075 x P

97] The Gear ratio required for cutting a screw thread of 25 mm on a lathe having a lead screw pitch using single point cutting tool is ----

A] 1:2

B] 2:1

C] 1:1 mm

98] A tumbler gear unit has

A] a single gear

B] two gears

C] three gears

D] four gears

99] Which one is the operation that cannot be done on the slotting machine?

A] key way slotting

B] dovetail slotting

C] gear cutting

D] thread cutting

100] The threads on the back side of the four Jaw chuck has type-----of threads

A] Square

3] Trapezoidal

C] V -shape

D] None of these

101] A voltage source produces an IR drop of 40V across a 20 ohms resistance, 60V across a 30 ohms resistance and 180V across a 90 ohms resistance all in series]How much is the applied voltage?

A] 180 V

B] 240 V

C] 100 V

D] 280 V

102] The initial function of a choke in a tube light circuit is to...

A] limit the starting current

B] induce high voltage

C] heat up the filament

D] limit the current after starting

103] The peak-to-peak voltage is 99V]how big is the effective value of the sine wave?

A] 70 V

B] 44.5V

C] 49.5 V

D] 35 V

104]A moving coil voltmeter reads 10 V AC]How big is the effective voltage?

A] higher

B] lower

C] the same

D]10% higher

105]A capacitor is connected across a 200 volt AC line, its minimum voltage rating should be...

A]100 volts

B] 200 Volts

C]300 volts

D]400 volts

106]How much is the nominal output voltage of a carbon zinc cell?

A]12V

B]1.5V

C]2.0V

D]2.2V

107]Cells are connected in series to..
A]increase the output voltage
B]decreases the output voltage
C]decrease the internal resistance
D]increase the current capacity
108] An unknown DC voltage is to be measured, which measuring range will you select first?
A]500V
B]50V
C]1.5 V
D]0.5V
109]Heat developed in a conductor is proportional to the...
A]square of the power
B]square of the resistance
C]square of the current
D]square of the time
110]The second function of a choke in a tube light circuit is to...
A]limit the starting current
B]induce high voltage
C]heat up the filament
D]limit the current after starting
111]A moving iron ammeter reads 10 A]how big is the peak current of the oscillation?
A]7.07 A
B]1.1414A
C]70.7 A
D]14.1 A
112]Power companies are interested in improving the power factor to
A]reduce line current
B]increase motor efficiency
C]increase volt-amperes
D]decrease power
113] In a RL parallel circuit, the opposition to total current is called...
A]reactance
B]resistance
C]a vector sum
D]impedance

114] An unknown direct current of micro ampere rating is to be measured, which measuring range will you select first?

A]20 micro amp

B]15 micro amp

C]150 micro amp

D]500 micro amp

115]The earth conductor provides a path to ground for..

A]leakage current

B]over current

C]high voltage

D]circuit current

116]Which appliance works on heating effect of electric current?

A]incandescent lamp

B]bimetallic thermostat

C]H R C fuse

D]toaster

117] External Thread provide on Rod or Pipe , by Die and Cutting Tool is called ......

(A] Tapping

(B] Dieing

(C] Threading

(D] Grooving

118] G.l pipes are provided externally with

A] no threads

B] parallel threads

C] tapered threads

D] neither parallel nor tapered threads.

119] in the pipe assembly, the hemp packing is used

A] for easy engagement

B] to fill the gap between threads

C] to avoid leakage

D] to get tight fitting.

120]The sealing compound shall be applied on the pipe threads

A] before hemp packing

B] after hemp packing

C] before and after temp packing

D] none of the above.

121] Used on finished tubular wrench surfaces to avoid marking]

A Stillson pipe

B] <u>Chain wrench</u>

C] Strap wrench

D] Footprint wrench

122] Used for gripping and turning pipes and round stocks in confined places]

A] Stillson pipe

B] Chain wrench

C] Strap wrench

D] <u>Footprint wrench</u>

123] Used for holding large diameter pipes]

A] Stillson pipe

B] <u>Chain wrench</u>

C] Strap wrench

D] Footprint wrench

124] Used for gripping and turning pipes,tubes and cylindricai rods]

A] <u>Stillson pipe</u>

B] Chain wrench

C] Strap wrench

D] Footprint wrench

125] Secures rope to small pipe or rim.

A] Slip knot

B] Bowline knot

C] Square knot

D] <u>Sheep shank knot</u>]

126] It can be folded and carried to any place] Similar to the quick releasing type pipe vice.

A <u>Portable folding pipe vice</u>

B] Chain pipe vice

C] Pipe vice

D] None of above

127] Used to hold pipes more than 63mm to 200mm diameter.

A] Portable folding pipe vice

B] <u>Chain pipe vice</u>

C] Pipe vice

D] None of above

128] Used for quick holding and locating pipes] Used to hold pipes up to 63mm diameter]

A] Portable folding pipe vice
B] Chain pipe vice
C] <u>Pipe vice</u>
D] None of above
129] Provides deviation of 90°
A] Plug
B] <u>Elbow</u>
C] Bend
D] Reducer 'T' branczh
130] Provides change of direction with a long radius at right angle.
A] Plug
B] Elbow
C] <u>Bend</u>
D] Reducer 'T' branczh
131] Used for closing a line which has an internal thread.
A] <u>Plug</u>
B] Elbow
C] Bend
D] Reducer 'T' branczh
132] Provides deviation of '45°
A] Bend
B] Reducer 'T' branczh
C] <u>Elbow</u>
D] Tee piece
133] Provides outlet at right angles to the run.
A] Bend
B] Reducer 'T' branczh
C] Elbow
D] <u>Tee piece</u>
134] Used where a change in ' pipe diameter is required]
A] Bend
B] <u>Reducer 'T' branczh</u>
C] Elbow
D] Tee piece
135] Selection of a former depends on the
A] <u>outside diameter of the pipe</u>
B] wall thickness of the pipe
C] bore diameter of the pipe

D] all the above.

136] A branch type hand operated pipe bending machine is used to bend

A] P.V.C.pipes

B] onduit pipes

C] <u>G.I.pipes</u>

D] copper pipes.

137] The inner formers of a hydraulic pipe bending machine are able to bend pipes up to a diameter of

A] 40mm

B] 100mm

C] 20mm

D] <u>75mm</u>

138] The included angle of a pipe thread is

A] 60°

B] 47°

C] <u>55°</u>

D] 45°

139] G.l.pipes are available in a standard length of

A] 5 metres

B] 18"

C] <u>6 metres</u>

D] 16 feet.

140] The standard pipe fittings are provided with threads conforming with

A] BA

B] BSW

C] <u>BSP</u>

D] Metric.

141] The external threads on G.l.pipes are out easily

A] by tap sets

B] <u>dies and die stocks</u>

C] centre lathes

D] thread rollers

142] Used where bolt and threads are to be protected from damage.

A] <u>Donald cap nut</u>

B] Thumb nut

C] Hexagonal nut

D] Wing-nut

143] Used where frequent removal and fixing is required.
A] Donald cap nut
B] Thumb nut
C] Hexagonal nut
D] <u>Wing-nut</u>
144] Used in machine building and structure work.
A] Donald cap nut
B] Thumb nut
C] <u>Hexagonal nut</u>
D] Wing-nut
145] Used where frequent adjustments are to be made.
A] Donald cap nut
B] <u>Thumb nut</u>
C] Hexagonal nut
D] Wing-nut
146] Nylon inserts in the nut prevent loosening.
A] Locking plate
B] Wire lock
C] <u>Self-locking nut</u>
D] Sawn nut
147] A slot is cut halfway across the nut.
A] Locking plate
B] Wire lock
C] Self-locking nut
D] <u>Sawn nut</u>
148] Prevents slackening of two bolts.
A] Locking plate
B] <u>Wire lock</u>
C] Self-locking nut
D] Sawn nut
149] Prevents rotation of the top nut.
A] <u>Lock-nut</u>
B] Grooved nut
C] Self-locking nut
D] Sawn nut
150] Prevents loosening of nut by the use of a plate shaped to fit the nut.
A] <u>Locking plate</u>
B] Wire lock

C] Self-locking nut

D] Sawn nut

151] Hexagonal nut with the lower part made cylindrical and the recessed groove.

A] Lock-nut

B] Grooved nut

C] Self-locking nut

D] Sawn nut

152] Drill a blind hole equal to half of the diameter of the stud. Insert this tool into the hole and remove the stud by turning this anticlockwise.

A] Prick Punch Method

B] Filing square very mm

C] Using square taper punch

D] Ezy-out method

153] If the stud is broken near to the surface, employ this method to remove the stud.

A] Prick Punch Method

B] Filing square very mm

C] Using square taper punch

D] Ezy-out method

154] When a stud is broken a little above the surface this method is used to remove the stud.

A] Filing square very mm

B] Using square taper punch

C] Ezy-out method

D] Making drill hole

155] To extract the broken stud a special tool is employed in this method.

A] Prick Punch Method

B] Filing square very mm

C] Using square taper punch

D] Ezy-out method

156] The inner formers of a hydraulic pipe bending machine are able to bend pipes up to a diameter of

A] 40mm

B] 100mm

C] 20mm

D] 75mm

157] Which is not the property of hydraulic fluid used in grinding machine?

A] it must not control or absorb air

B] it must not cause corrosion of the moving parts

C] Should have adequate viscosity

D] it must vaporize at the operating temperature

158] Which one of the following is the advantage of pneumatic system?

A] For low cost layout

B] For increasing the rate of production

C] For better working environment

159] Following which advantage of Pneumatic power system

A] For increase production rate.

B] Less cash for layout

C] Good climate for work

D] Above all

160]The pressure of fluid in hydraulic brake system is governed by

A] boils law

B] Charles law

C] Pascal's law

D] none of the above laws

161] Allows fluid both way in and out of cylinder

A] Piston

B] Push Rod

C] Primary cup

D] Check valve

162] Relieves excess pressure of air from the air tank]

A] Air compressor

B] Unloader valve

C] Safety valve

D] Brake chamber

163] Regulates maximum air pressure, reaching to air tank]

A] Air compressor

B] Unloader valve

C] Safety valve

D] Brake chamber

164] Distributes air to various circuits

A] Brake actuator

B] Dual brake valve

C] <u>System protection valve</u>

165] Develops pressure on fuel to go out

A] Valves

B] Coil spring

C] <u>Diaphragm</u>

D] Rocker arm

166] Takes thrust load

A] Crankshaft

B] Flywheels

C] Torque wrench

D] <u>Thrust bearing</u>

167] Only spur gears are used

A] <u>Sliding mesh</u>

B] Synchromesh

C] Double declutching

D] Transfer case

168] Used for smooth gear shifting

A] Sliding mesh

B] Synchromesh

C] <u>Double declutching</u>

D] Transfer case

169] Hard gear shifting is due to

A] Worn out clutch disc

B] Damaged main shaft bearings

C] <u>Synchronizer unit damaged</u>

D] excessive oil in the gearbox.

170] Gear slip is due to

A] <u>Worn out synchroniser</u>

B] Worn out clutch disc

C] Dry main shaft bearing

D] Weak pressure spring of clutch.

171] Noise in particular gear is due to

A] Insufficient clutch pedal free play

B] Damage gear teeth

C] Cracked gear box case

D] <u>Damaged synchromesh unit</u>.

Thank You

Thank You for reading this Book.

25